A Little Jar of Oil

The Story of Elisha and the Widow

We are grateful to the following team of authors for their contributions to *God Loves Me*, a Bible story program for young children. This Bible story, one of a series of fifty-two, was written by Patricia L. Nederveld, managing editor for CRC Publications. Suggestions for using this book were developed by Jesslyn DeBoer, a freelance author from Grand Rapids, Michigan. Yvonne Van Ee, an early childhood educator, served as project consultant and wrote *God Loves Me*, the program guide that accompanies this series of Bible storybooks.

Nederveld has served as a consultant to Title I early childhood programs in Colorado. She has extensive experience as a writer, teacher, and consultant for federally funded preschool, kindergarten, and early childhood programs in Colorado, Texas, Michigan, Florida, Missouri, and Washington, using the *High/Scope* Education Research Foundation curriculum. In addition to writing the *Bible Footprints* church curriculum for four- and five-year-olds, Nederveld edited the revised *Threes* curriculum and the first edition of preschool through second grade materials for the *LiFE* curriculum, all published by CRC Publications.

DeBoer has served as a church preschool leader and as coauthor of the preschool-kindergarten materials for the *LiFE* curriculum published by CRC Publications. She has also written K-6 science and health curriculum for Christian Schools International, Grand Rapids, Michigan, and inspirational gift books for Zondervan Publishing House.

Van Ee is a professor and early childhood program advisor in the Education Department at Calvin College, Grand Rapids, Michigan. She has served as curriculum author and consultant for Christian Schools International and wrote the original *Story Hour* organization manual and curriculum materials for fours and fives.

Photo on page 5: Frank Herholdt/Tony Stone Images; photo on page 20: Martin Chaffer/Tony Stone Images.

Library of Congress Cataloging-in-Publication Data

Nederveld, Patricia L., 1944-
     A little jar of oil: the story of Elisha and widow/Patricia L. Nederveld.
       p. cm. — (God loves me; bk. 20)
     Summary: Retells the Bible story of Elisha and the poor widow, whose
little jar of oil fills many jars with oil. Includes follow-up activities.
     ISBN 1-56212-289-4
     1. Elisha (Biblical prophet)—Juvenile literature. 2. Bible stories, English
—O.T. Samuel, 1st. 4. Bible games and puzzles. [1. Elisha (Biblical prophet)
2. Bible stories—O.T.] I. Title. II. Series: Nederveld, Patricia L., 1944-
God loves me; bk. 20.
BS580.E5N43 1998
222'.5409505—dc21
                                    97-32478
                                       CIP
                                       AC

10 9 8 7 6 5 4 3 2 1

A Little Jar of Oil
The Story of Elisha and the Widow

PATRICIA L. NEDERVELD

ILLUSTRATIONS BY LISA WORKMAN

CRC Publications
Grand Rapids, Michigan

This is a story
from God's
book, the Bible.

It's for say name(s) of
your child(ren).
It's for me too!

2 Kings 4:1-7

Long ago, in the land of God's people, there lived a mommy and two boys. They had no daddy. That made them very sad. They had no food either. That made them very hungry!

The mommy went to talk to Elisha, the man of God. "Elisha, my family is hungry! But I have no money to buy food for them. What shall I do?"

Elisha saw the mommy's tears, and he felt sorry for her. "What *do* you have in your house?" he asked.

"Just one small jar filled with cooking oil," said the mommy.

"Well," said Elisha, "here's what you must do. . . ."

"Go and find as many empty jars as you can. Ask your friends! Ask your neighbors! Ask everyone! Then line up all the jars on your table and pour them full of oil from your little jar. . . ."

Can you see what God did? One, two, three, four—and lots more! God made sure the oil from that one little jar kept pouring until every jar was filled!

The mommy ran back to tell Elisha about the amazing thing God did. "Now you can sell all those jars of oil and buy food for your family!" said Elisha with a smile.

And that's just
what she did!

I wonder if you know that our food comes from God . . .

Dear God, thank you for taking such good care of us. We're so glad you give us food every day! Amen.

Suggestions for Follow-up

Opening

Greet your little ones with a cheerful smile and a reminder that God loves each one.

Gather your children in a circle or sit around a low table. Ask them if they are hungry—most little ones will say yes! Offer nutritious snack foods (small crackers, halved grapes, cheese cubes) in small baskets or plastic bowls. Talk about the shapes and colors and flavors of the food. Remind your little ones that God gives them this good food. Invite them to fold their hands and give God thanks as you say this prayer:

> *God is great, and God is good.*
> *Let us thank him for this food. Amen.*
> —Anonymous

If you wish, sing the prayer (music in Songs Section, *God Loves Me* program guide).

Learning Through Play

Learning through play is the best way! The following activity suggestions are meant to help you provide props and experiences that will invite the children to play their way into the Scripture story and its simple truth. Try to provide plenty of time for the children to choose their own activities and to play individually. Use group activities sparingly—little ones learn most comfortably with a minimum of structure.

1. Invite your children to make food collage mobiles. Provide glue sticks, paper plates, and pictures of food cut from magazine and grocery store circulars. Let the children select pictures, and show them how to glue them to one side of the plate. Provide copies of the "God is great . . ." prayer card (see Pattern G, Patterns Section, *God Loves Me* program guide), and show the children how to glue the prayer on the other side of the plate. Punch a hole near the top of the plate, and loop a 24" (61 cm) length of yarn through the hole; tie the ends to form a hanger. Encourage the children to ask Mom or Dad to hang the mobile above their kitchen table to remind them to thank God for the good food God gives them every day.

2. Set up a kitchen with dishes, pots and pans, small plastic containers, and toy food or dry nonsweetened cereal, soup crackers, raisins, and tiny M&M candies. You might want to set up a grocery store nearby with grocery bags and empty boxes and cans. Cook and shop with your little ones, and talk about the good food God gives us. Model praise and prayers for these gifts and for God's care.

3. Children may be curious about the oil in the story. Bring a bottle of cooking oil, and pour some into a paper cup. Show them how the oil soaks through the paper and makes the cup look greasy. Pour some onto a napkin or paper towel, and watch the paper absorb the oil. Pour small amounts of oil on the waxed side of freezer wrap, and let the children finger paint greasy designs. Dab a bit of oil on each child's pointer finger, and invite the children to taste it (you might want to use melted butter or oleo for a better flavor). Explain that oil is mixed with other foods like sugar and eggs and flour

to make pancakes, bread, and cookies. If you have time, prepare a package of muffin mix, adding the oil and other ingredients. (You'll have eager helpers!) Tell your little ones that oil is a very valuable food. The widow was very thankful for the oil God gave her. She could sell it to buy other food for her boys.

4. Set up a water table with small plastic pails or dishpans full of water. Cover the table with a plastic shower curtain liner, and keep a mop or paper towels handy for wiping up spills. Provide various sizes and types of plastic containers for dipping and pouring. As your little ones pour the water from one container to another, talk about how much water each will hold. Help children build concepts about volume—ask if the container is full or empty, and notice which ones hold the most. Act out the roles of the mother and her sons, filling jar after jar with "oil." Together count the "jars of oil" as you fill them.

5. Use popcorn to show how God can change the smallest amounts of food into quantities large enough to share. Show the children how few kernels you need to prepare this snack. As children watch you pop the kernels in an air popper, make sure little hands cannot reach the hot popper or popped kernels. You may want to dribble a little oil (melted butter or oleo) over the popcorn. Give each child a small cupful of the fluffiest popped corn. Talk about how God made this food so tasty and how the kernels changed from a very little handful into a big

bowl of popcorn. Imagine with the children how surprised the widow and her two boys must have been when one small jar of oil kept filling so many jars.

Closing

Sing several of these stanzas of "God Is So Good" (Songs Section, *God Loves Me* program guide) as children follow your actions:

> *God is so good* . . . (point up)
> *He cares for me* . . . (point to self)
> *God gives me food* . . . (point up)
> *Thank you, dear God* . . . (fold hands; sing prayer)
> —Words: Stanza 1 and 2, traditional

Place an apple or heart sticker on each child's hand as they leave, and whisper a reminder about God's love.

At Home

Use our little ones appreciation of daily routines to establish the habit of prayer. Begin by modeling prayers at mealtime. You may wish to teach your child one or more simple prayers of thankfulness for food like the one in this book. Whether your child prefers to compose words or recite a memorized prayer, encourage your little one to take a turn leading the family in the mealtime prayer. A bedtime prayer routine can signal to your child that it is time to rest. If your child prefers to quiet down with music, sing a prayer together.

Old Testament Stories

Blue and Green and Purple Too! *The Story of God's Colorful World*

It's a Noisy Place! *The Story of the First Creatures*

Adam and Eve *The Story of the First Man and Woman*

Take Good Care of My World! *The Story of Adam and Eve in the Garden*

A Very Sad Day *The Story of Adam and Eve's Disobedience*

A Rainy, Rainy Day *The Story of Noah*

Count the Stars! *The Story of God's Promise to Abraham and Sarah*

A Girl Named Rebekah *The Story of God's Answer to Abraham*

Two Coats for Joseph *The Story of Young Joseph*

Plenty to Eat *The Story of Joseph and His Brothers*

Safe in a Basket *The Story of Baby Moses*

I'll Do It! *The Story of Moses and the Burning Bush*

Safe at Last! *The Story of Moses and the Red Sea*

What Is It? *The Story of Manna in the Desert*

A Tall Wall *The Story of Jericho*

A Baby for Hannah *The Story of an Answered Prayer*

Samuel! Samuel! *The Story of God's Call to Samuel*

Lions and Bears! *The Story of David the Shepherd Boy*

David and the Giant *The Story of David and Goliath*

A Little Jar of Oil *The Story of Elisha and the Widow*

One, Two, Three, Four, Five, Six, Seven! *The Story of Elisha and Naaman*

A Big Fish Story *The Story of Jonah*

Lions, Lions! *The Story of Daniel*

New Testament Stories

Jesus Is Born! *The Story of Christmas*

Good News! *The Story of the Shepherds*

An Amazing Star! *The Story of the Wise Men*

Waiting, Waiting, Waiting! *The Story of Simeon and Anna*

Who Is This Child? *The Story of Jesus in the Temple*

Follow Me! *The Story of Jesus and His Twelve Helpers*

The Greatest Gift *The Story of Jesus and the Woman at the Well*

A Father's Wish *The Story of Jesus and a Little Boy*

Just Believe! *The Story of Jesus and a Little Girl*

Get Up and Walk! *The Story of Jesus and a Man Who Couldn't Walk*

A Little Lunch *The Story of Jesus and a Hungry Crowd*

A Scary Storm *The Story of Jesus and a Stormy Sea*

Thank You, Jesus! *The Story of Jesus and One Thankful Man*

A Wonderful Sight! *The Story of Jesus and a Man Who Couldn't See*

A Better Thing to Do *The Story of Jesus and Mary and Martha*

A Lost Lamb *The Story of the Good Shepherd*

Come to Me! *The Story of Jesus and the Children*

Have a Great Day! *The Story of Jesus and Zacchaeus*

I Love You, Jesus! *The Story of Mary's Gift to Jesus*

Hosanna! *The Story of Palm Sunday*

The Best Day Ever! *The Story of Easter*

Goodbye—for Now *The Story of Jesus' Return to Heaven*

A Prayer for Peter *The Story of Peter in Prison*

Sad Day, Happy Day! *The Story of Peter and Dorcas*

A New Friend *The Story of Paul's Conversion*

Over the Wall *The Story of Paul's Escape in a Basket*

A Song in the Night *The Story of Paul and Silas in Prison*

A Ride in the Night *The Story of Paul's Escape on Horseback*

The Shipwreck *The Story of Paul's Rescue at Sea*

Holiday Stories

Selected stories from the New Testament to help you celebrate the Christian year

Jesus Is Born! *The Story of Christmas*

Good News! *The Story of the Shepherds*

An Amazing Star! *The Story of the Wise Men*

Hosanna! *The Story of Palm Sunday*

The Best Day Ever! *The Story of Easter*

Goodbye—for Now *The Story of Jesus' Return to Heaven*

These fifty-two books are the heart of *God Loves Me,* a Bible story program designed for young children. Individual books (or the entire set) and the accompanying program guide *God Loves Me* are available from CRC Publications (1-800-333-8300).